AFRICAN FOOD SECURITY URBAN NETWORK (AFSUN)
SOUTHERN AFRICAN MIGRATION PROGRAMME (SAMP)

MIGRATION, DEVELOPMENT AND URBAN FOOD SECURITY

JONATHAN CRUSH

SERIES EDITOR: JONATHAN CRUSH

URBAN FOOD SECURITY SERIES NO. 9

ACKNOWLEDGEMENTS

The financial support of the Canadian Government for AFSUN through the CIDA UPCD Tier One program is acknowledged, as is the support of IDRC and OSISA for SAMP. The assistance of Cassandra Eberhardt, Bruce Frayne, Jane Battersby, Godfrey Tawodzera and Wade Pendleton is acknowledged. This report has also been published as SAMP Migration Policy Series No. 60.

Cover Photograph: Peter Mackenzie for SAMP

© *AFSUN 2012, SAMP 2012*

ISBN 978-1-920409-78-4

First published 2012

Production by Bronwen Müller, Cape Town

AUTHOR

Jonathan Crush is the Co-Director of AFSUN, Director of the Southern African Research Centre at Queen's University and CIGI Research Chair in Global Migration and Development at the Balsillie School for International Affairs. He also holds an Honorary Professorship at the University of Cape Town.

Previous Publications in the AFSUN Series

Contents

FIGURES

TABLES

1. INTRODUCTION

Over the last decade, two issues have risen to the top of the international development agenda: (a) Food Security; and (b) Migration and Development. Each has its own international agency champions (the FAO and the IOM), its own international gatherings (the Global Forum on International Migration and the World Forum on Food Security), its own national line ministries (Departments of Immigration and Home Affairs and Departments of Agriculture and Food Security) and its own voluminous body of research and scholarly publications. Some international organizations (such as the World Bank) deal with both issues but in such separate silos that they might as well be in separate organizations. There is, in other words, a massive institutional and substantive disconnect between these two development agendas. The reasons are hard to understand since the connections between migration and food security seem obvious. Indeed, one cannot be properly understood and addressed independently of the other.

Global and regional discussions about the relationship between migration and development cover a broad range of policy issues including remittance flows, the brain drain, the role of diasporas and return migration.[1] Strikingly absent from these discussions is any systematic discussion of the relationship between population migration and food security. There are a number of possible reasons for this. First, discussions of the impact of migration on development tend to be pitched at the global and national scale and focus on economic growth and productive investment. Secondly, when discussion turns to the household level, the debate focuses largely on remittance flows and the use of remittances by the household. There is a general consensus that the expenditure of remittances on basic livelihood needs is somehow non-developmental in that it does not lead to investment and sustainable productive activity.[2] Not only is this an extremely narrow perspective, it also means that the food needs of households (and their food security more generally) are rarely given much consideration as development objectives and outcomes. Thirdly, while this debate does seek to understand the drivers of migration, it seems to ignore food shortages and insecurity as a basic cause of migration and it certainly seems to forget that migrants themselves have to eat in the towns and cities to which they migrate. Finally, discussions of migration and development tend to focus more on international than internal migration. Food security is certainly affected by international migration (for example, households in Zimbabwe rely heavily on remittances from around the world to purchase food and other necessities). However, the relationship between migration and food security is particularly important within national boundaries.

If the global migration and development debate sidelines food security, the current international food security agenda has a similar disregard for migration. The primary focus of the agenda is food insecurity and under-nutrition and how enhanced agricultural production by small farmers can resolve these endemic problems.[3] The influential Alliance for a Green Revolution in Africa (AGRA), for example, was established "to achieve a food secure and prosperous Africa through the promotion of rapid, sustainable agricultural growth based on smallholder farmers."[4] In much of the thinking about rural food insecurity, there is an implicit assumption that Africa's rural areas are bounded territories whose main problem is that households do not produce enough food for themselves.

By drawing boundaries around the "rural" in this way, there is a tendency to ignore the reality that migration is a critical food security strategy for rural households up and down the African continent. Any intervention to try and improve the food security of rural populations therefore needs to acknowledge that migration both deprives rural households of agricultural labour and provides them with the remittances to purchase agricultural inputs and foodstuffs. Rural households purchase a good deal of their food with cash that they receive from absent household members who are working in other parts of a country or in other countries altogether. Rural food insecurity is therefore not simply about how much a household produces from the land; often it is more about the fact that remittances from migrants are too small or too irregular to allow households to purchase sufficient, good quality food.

If migration is a neglected aspect of discussions about rural food insecurity, it is almost totally absent from considerations of the causes and impact of food security amongst urban populations. Many poor urban households in African cities are made up entirely or partially of migrants. Rural to urban migration is rarely a one-way, one-time move, however. Many urban dwellers speak of and feel attached to a rural home. Households in Africa are often spatially stretched between rural and urban spaces and occupied by different members of the kin group at different times. The reality on the ground, then, is that the distinction between "the rural" and "the urban" is an "obsolete dichotomy" in Africa.[5] As Ellis and Harris maintain: "It is not very helpful to treat 'rural areas' as undifferentiated territories that exhibit definitively distinct features from 'urban areas.'"[6] Households are not static self-contained rural or urban units but fluid entities with permeable boundaries whose degree of food security is constantly and profoundly shaped by the mobility of people in a continent "on the move."[7] If we accept this general argument, it immediately becomes clear that it would be unwise to drive a wedge between rural and urban food security as if they had very little relationship to or impact on one another. On the contrary, not only are they inter-related but migration becomes an important key to unlocking this relationship.[8]

In summary, food security needs to be "mainstreamed" into the migration and development agenda and migration needs to be "mainstreamed" into the food security agenda.[9] Without such an effort, both agendas will proceed in ignorance of the other to the detriment of both. The result will be a singular failure to understand, and manage, the crucial reciprocal relationship between migration and food security. This paper sets out to promote a conversation between the food security and migration agendas in the African context in the light of what we know and what we need to know about their connections. Four main issues are singled out for attention: (a) the relationship between internal migration and urban food security; (b) the relationship between international migration and urban food security; (d) the difference in food security between migrant and non-migrant urban households; and (d) the role of rural-urban food transfers in urban food security. Prior to addressing these issues, it is important to disaggregate the complex phenomenon of migration not least because it has been undergoing dramatic change in Africa.

2. INTERNAL MIGRATION AND URBAN FOOD SECURITY

2.1 Urbanization and Circulation

Rapid urbanization is a distinguishing characteristic of contemporary Africa and a great deal of this urban growth is fuelled by rural-urban migration. The urban population of SADC increased from 20.5 million in 1990 to an estimated 34 million in 2010 (Table 1).[10] UN-HABITAT predicts that it will increase further to 39 million in 2020 and 52 million in 2030. At the present time, 59% of the population is urbanized, a figure

TABLE 1: Southern African Urban Population, 1950-2050											
Population	1950	1960	1970	1980	1990	2000	2010	2020	2030	2040	2050
Urban (000s)	5,869	8,277	11,118	14,752	20,502	27,657	34,021	38,809	43,741	48,119	51,917
Urban (%)	37.7	42.0	43.7	44.7	48.8	53.8	58.7	63.5	68.3	72.9	75.0
All Africa (%)	14.4	18.6	23.6	27.9	32.1	35.9	39.9	44.6	49.9	55.7	61.6
Source: State of African Cities 2010											

projected to pass 70% in the next 20 years and to rise to over 75% by mid-century (Figure 1).

FIGURE 1: Southern African Urban Population, 1950-2050

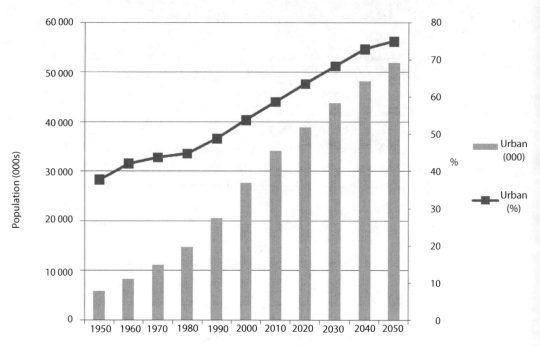

In 1990, only South Africa was more than 50% urbanized. By 2050, all of the region's countries except Swaziland are projected to be over 50% urbanized (Table 2). Urbanization rates will exceed 75% in Angola, Botswana and South Africa. Evidence for rapid urbanization in Africa should not be interpreted as a permanent one-time rural-to-urban shift or that rural areas are undergoing an inevitable process of depopulation. Certainly the overall trend is towards more people living for longer periods in towns and cities. But this does not mean that they are necessarily cutting all links to the countryside. Indeed, there is considerable evidence that most first-generation migrants retain very close ties with their rural homesteads. This adds considerable complexity to our understanding of migration dynamics and impacts.

TABLE 2: Southern African Urbanisation, 1950-2050 (% Urbanised)										
Country	1950	1960	1970	1980	1990	2000	2010	2020	2030	2040	2050
Angola	7.6	10.4	15.0	24.3	37.1	49.0	58.5	66.0	71.6	76.4	80.5
Botswana	2.7	3.1	7.8	16.5	41.9	53.2	61.1	67.6	72.7	77.1	81.7
Lesotho	1.4	3.4	8.6	11.5	14.0	20.0	26.9	34.6	42.4	50.2	58.1
Mozambique	2.4	3.7	5.8	13.1	21.1	30.7	38.4	46.3	53.7	60.8	67.4
Namibia	13.4	17.9	22.3	25.1	27.7	32.4	38.0	44.4	51.5	58.6	65.3
South Africa	42.2	46.6	47.8	48.4	52.0	56.9	61.7	66.6	71.3	75.7	79.6
Swaziland	1.8	3.9	9.7	17.9	22.9	22.6	21.4	22.3	26.2	32.5	39.5
Zambia	11.5	18.2	30.4	39.8	39.4	34.8	35.7	38.9	44.7	51.6	53.4
Zimbabwe	10.6	12.6	17.4	22.4	29.0	33.8	38.3	43.9	50.7	57.7	64.4
Source: State of African Cities 2010										

South Africa has the highest proportion of urban dwellers of all SADC countries (60-70%) and appears closest to the model of a classic "urban transition."[11] A progressively greater proportion of the population lives permanently in towns and cities, not least because the rural areas of the country do not offer households the prospect of a decent livelihood or many future prospects.[12] The volume of internal migration in South Africa grew rapidly after the collapse of apartheid-era influx controls.[13] Cumulative migration (the number of people living in a province other than their province of birth) was 5.5 million in 2001, or more than 10% of the total South African-born population. Internal migration (whether of population in general or of temporary labour migrants) is therefore an extremely significant phenomenon in South Africa. At the municipal level, most internal migration is towards municipalities that are highly urbanized (the so-called 'metros'). The South African Cities Network calculated that the seven largest urban municipalities in South Africa attracted over 500,000 additional migrants between 2001 and 2006.[14] In five of those areas, these migrants made up over 4% of the total population (Table 3).

TABLE 3: South African Municipalities Experiencing Greatest In-Migration, 2001-6				
Name of Municipality	Province	Net In-Migration	Total Pop. in 2006	Recent In-Migrants as % of Total Pop.
Ekurhuleni	Gauteng	140,252	2,384,020	5.9
City of Tshwane	Gauteng	137,685	1,926,214	7.1
City of Cape Town	Western Cape	129,400	2,952,385	4.4
City of Johannesburg	Gauteng	120,330	2,993,716	4.0
West Rand	Gauteng	42,674	732,759	5.8
eThekwini	KwaZulu-Natal	27,277	2,978,811	0.9
Nelson Mandela	Eastern Cape	6,715	1,073,114	0.6
Source: State of the Cities Report 2006, p. 2.18.				

Simply because urbanization is proceeding rapidly, it does not mean that individuals or households who move are cutting their links with rural areas. How significant a phenomenon is circular migration in South Africa and, if so, is it likely to continue?[15] The answers to these questions have a significant bearing on both rural and urban food security in the country. Based on their work in rural and peri-urban communities in the eastern part of the country, Collinson et al argue for the existence of "highly prevalent circular migration" between rural and urban areas and note a marked increase in temporary female migration.[16] While there does seem to be a trend towards greater permanent migration of households to urban areas, temporary labour migration from rural households did grow after the end of apartheid. The number of rural households with members who were migrant workers actually increased in the 1990s and a significant proportion of households are reliant on migrant remittances. In 1993, 33% of all rural households reported at least one migrant member. By 2002, this figure had increased to 38% (an increase of 300,000 households).[17] In the last decade, however, it appears that the number of households with migrant workers may have begun to fall as migrants (and households) settle more permanently in urban areas.[18] The number of households with an absent adult member, for example, dropped from 2.2 million in 1993 to 1.6 million in 2008 (a fall to 30% of all households).

Zambia represents a rather different model of the relationship between internal migration and urbanization. The nature of urbanization in Zambia has been a source of debate for years.[19] Zambia's urban population grew from 3.2 million in 1990 to 3.6 million in 2000. However, the proportion of the population living in urban areas actually fell from 39% to 35%, prompting researchers to conclude that growing economic hardship and urban poverty was leading to a process of "counter-urbanization."[20] As Potts concludes, "while the fact of net out-migration from urban areas during the 1990s has now been established as a component in the drop in urbanisation levels, it is possible to now state that it was the primary component".[21] Zambia's post-2000 economic recovery and growth may well have reversed the counter-urbanization trend of the 1990s. Certainly this is the view of UN-HABITAT which estimates that urban growth rates increased from 1.1% per annum between 1995 and 2000 to 2.3% per annum between 2005 and 2010. Zambia's Central Statistical Office notes a recent increase in rural-rural and rural-urban migration and a decline in urban-rural migration (Figure 2).[22] However, there is every indication that rural-urban linkages remain strong in Zambia and will remain that way into the foreseeable future.

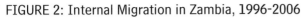

FIGURE 2: Internal Migration in Zambia, 1996-2006

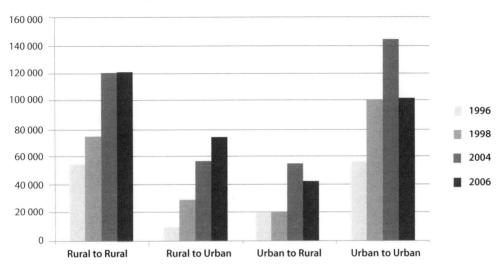

Source: Ianchovichina and Lundstrom, Inclusive Growth in Zambia, p. 4.

Zimbabwe presents a third scenario in which political and economic crisis have precipitated major shifts in internal population movement. During a relatively prosperous first decade of independence after 1981, rural–urban migration increased rapidly as people sought new economic opportunities in the country's towns and cities.[23] Most new urbanites maintained close contact with their rural roots and circular migration was fairly typical.[24] In the 1990s, the country's Structural Economic Programme (SAP) slowed both the post-independence economic boom and the pace of urbaniza-tion.[25] Unemployment began to increase but the urban population still increased by over 1 million between 1990 and 2000 (and from 29% to 34% of the total population). The crisis in the formal urban job market and the serious decline in urban incomes led to net out-migration from the main towns.[26]

Draconian government policies caused further livelihood destruction and internal migration. The forcible expropriation of white-owned commer-cial farms led to massive displacement of black farmworkers to the towns. That was followed by Operation Murambatsvina, "a lethal mixture of vindictive electoral politics, a particularly strong attachment to planned environments, and a wish to reduce the urban population for political and economic reasons."[27] The nationwide assault on urban informality destroyed the housing and livelihoods of hundreds of thousands of urban households.[28] However, it was not particularly successful in its aim of forcing urban-dwellers to retreat permanently into the rural areas. The major difference with Zambia in the 1990s was that many households, both rural and urban, turned to international migration as a survival strategy.[29]

Deborah Potts has recently reviewed the empirical evidence on urbanization trends in Sub-Saharan Africa and argues that the idea that migration is a permanent move to urban areas is misplaced.[30] Drawing on a range of empirical sources, and her own longitudinal tracking of migration trends in Zimbabwe, she argues that "circulation" between rural and urban areas is still a defining characteristic of African urbanization and internal migration:

> Circular migration between rural and urban areas remains a crucial, and adaptable, aspect of urbanization processes in sub-Saharan Africa... The scale, duration and direction of such migration flows have adapted in logical ways to the increasing poverty in urban areas that accompanied structural adjustment, and net in-migration has been reduced, sometimes very markedly. These adaptations are mainly the result of very negative livelihood changes for most of the urban population for whom there is no economic safety net, if all else fails, except within the nexus of rural-urban linkages.[31]

Various household surveys by Potts and others suggest that the dynamics of urbanization, circular migration and rural-urban linkage are complex and highly variable. As Potts notes, "migrants in town include different types of people with different histories, aspirations and social connections with their place of origin."[32]

Given the high rates of urbanisation in Southern Africa, migrants have a visible presence in the region's towns and cities. AFSUN's urban food security baseline survey in 2008-9 found that poor neighbourhoods in most cities were dominated by migrants.[33] Of the 6,453 urban households interviewed in 11 SADC cities, 38% were first-generation migrant households (that is, every member of the household was born outside the city). In contrast, only 13% of households had no migrant members. The remainder (nearly half) comprised a mix of migrants and non-migrants, usually households in which the adults were migrants and the children were born in the city. The relative importance of migrants did vary from city to city, however. All of the cities had a comparatively small proportion of non-migrant households (ranging from a low of 5% in the case of Gaborone to a high of 20% in the case of Johannesburg). In other words, in every city 80% or more of the households were composed either entirely of migrants or had some migrant members. The biggest difference was in the relative number of migrant households (from a high of 67% in Gaborone to a low of 9% in Harare).

At a general level these differences are attributable to each country's distinctive history of urbanisation. The four ex-apartheid cities (Cape Town, Johannesburg, Msunduzi and Windhoek) all have relatively high numbers of pure migrant households, a pattern that is broadly consistent with mass rural to urban household migration following the collapse of apartheid. Cities in countries that have been independent for a longer period (such as Malawi, Swaziland and Zambia) tend to have more mixed households and fewer purely migrant households. In those countries, independence was accompanied by rapid in-migration to primate cities and those urbanites have been in the cities long enough to have second and even third generation members born in the city. Mozambique and Zimbabwe became independent rather later and were also severely affected by pre-independence civil conflict and post-independence economic crisis. These two cities have an extraordinarily high number of mixed households (nearly 80%). The obvious anomaly in the survey is Gaborone with two thirds of its households consisting entirely of migrants. Gaborone has been urbanizing much faster than the either Manzini or Maseru (with which it is often compared) (see Table 4), a reflection of the fact that Botswana's economy is much more vibrant that Lesotho or Swaziland's, drawing more migrant households from the countryside to the city.

TABLE 4: Proportion of Migrant and Non-Migrant Households		
City	Migrant Households (% of Total)	Mixed Households (% of Total)	Non-Migrant Households (% of Total)
Gaborone	67	28	5
Cape Town	54	40	6
Msunduzi	48	43	9
Windhoek	49	40	11
Johannesburg	42	35	23
Maseru	37	52	11
Manzini	32	55	13
Lusaka	24	56	20
Blantyre	17	65	18
Maputo	11	78	11
Harare	9	78	13
Total	38	49	13

2.2 Food Security and Stretched Households

The rural focus of the international and national food security agenda is already influencing the way in which the migration-food security nexus is understood. A recent issue of the journal *Food Policy*, for example, suggests that "the sending of a migrant means the loss or reduced presence of one or more members of the household. On the consumption side this clearly means fewer mouths to feed and to support in other ways. On the production side, migration means the loss of labor and, in fact, the negative consequences of migration on nutrition are likely to come through this labor loss."[34] The major positive impact of migration is the remittances sent home by the migrant which can have direct and indirect effects on production and consumption.[35] Implicit in this analysis is a prioritisation of the impact of migration on the food security of the rural household. This is an important issue, but so is the relationship between migration and the food security of the urban household. A focus on migrant remittances will break the conventional notion of the rural household as wholly or mainly dependent on smallholder production, but it does not take us far enough in addressing the full range of impacts that migration has on food security, including the food security of the permanent and temporary residents of the region's towns and cities.

Rapid urbanization certainly effects massive change in the volume and nature of what a growing city eats. However, conceptualizations of migration and food security need to take account of the reality of "highly mobile urban and rural populations, coupled with complex, fluid households."[36] The concept of the "stretched household" seems most relevant to breaking down the artificial wall between the urban and the rural and between rural and urban food security. First, it more closely approximates a reality in which migrants "continue to be members of rural households whilst forming or joining other households in an urban area."[37] Secondly, it emphasizes the complex connections between the urban and the rural:

> The notion of a "divide" (between the rural and the urban) has become a misleading metaphor, one that oversimplifies and even distorts realities... The linkages and interactions have become an ever more intensive and important component of livelihoods and production systems in many areas – forming not so much a bridge over a divide as a complex web of connections in a landscape where much is neither "urban" nor "rural."[38]

Thirdly, the concept highlights the fact that urban and rural food security are often inter-dependent at the level of the individual household.

As urban-urban migration increases (for example, from smaller urban centres to large cities) within countries and across borders, "stretched households" are also emerging in the purely urban context. In Lesotho, for example, many households in the capital city of Maseru have members working in South African towns and cities. The National Migration

Survey in Namibia found that urban–urban migration made up 20% of lifetime migration moves.[39] In South Africa, the "fluidity, porosity and spatially 'stretched' nature of households" has been observed. Household fluidity relates to the "contested nature" of household membership, the claims of non-core urban household members on household resources and the "spatially extended nature of the links and resource flows thus created."[40] As a result, the density of exchanges between the two (primarily of people, goods, cash and social grants) impacts on the food security of stretched households:

> These (migrant) exchanges, networks and resource flows play a key role in alleviating the effects of poverty and managing vulnerability. They help households and household members to take advantage of opportunities and to diffuse risk across space. Ties to urban beneficiaries are a vital source of income for rural households in the context of ever-present monetisation and when living even in the countryside requires cash. For urban dwellers, the possibility of entitlements from rural households serves as a vital livelihood 'cushion', particularly if the rural kin have access to land or are able to care for children while parents seek employment in urban centres.[41]

Increasingly, multi-nodal households are emerging, "stretched" between two or more locations. In Maputo, poor urban households are stretched to include the Mozambican countryside and urban areas in South Africa:

> The urban poor in Maputo survive through a variety of strategies. The use of kinship networks is a principal strategy, in which 'non-market solidarities' are activated in the face of the failure of the state. The development of multiple household strategies, and the dispersal of family members geographically is one such strategy. A network of exchanges is developed between the households, with members in town exchanging goods and services with households in the countryside. Members of the family may migrate to neighbouring countries such as South Africa in order to spread the risk and diversify the sources of survival. Faced with the exigencies of survival there is a tension between the need for family cohesion and the pull of dispersal. The dissolution of traditional social bonds has been a cause of enormous insecurity and social vulnerability.[42]

Even in a small country like Lesotho, household members are dispersed by migration yet maintain strong social and material links with one another:

> The Basotho are integrated together in a fluid shifting ensemble of people, where members of the same family may have a relative managing sheep and goats in the upper Senqu Valley in Lesotho, while his brother cultivates mountain wheat and keeps a home ready for the

herdsman when he comes down for the winter. They have a sister who has married in the lowlands, where she struggles to grow maize on an exhausted piece of eroded land. Her husband is fortunate to work in the South African mines, and comes home monthly. When he was younger he brought cattle back home from the mines, but now as he has grown older he prefers to bring money and food and household goods. Most of his remittances are spent on food, clothing, education and medical expenses. They have another brother who teaches school in a peri-urban community near Mafeteng and two younger sisters: one who works as a domestic in Durban, South Africa, and another who works in a textile factory in Maseru. Both support themselves but also send money home. The sister recently married a policeman in the city of Bloemfontein, South Africa, and is waiting until he finds a place for both of them so she can move there. An uncle in Bloemfontein who took permanent residence in South Africa when he retired from the mines is helping them find a place to live. All of these folk visit each other regularly, so that there is a constant flow from mountain to lowland to town to South African city and back.[43]

In other words, a "household" may well have migrant members living, working and otherwise making do in more than one city in the country or region. This adds yet another layer of complexity and fluidity to household food security strategies.

3. SOUTH–SOUTH MIGRATION AND FOOD SECURITY

3.1 Changing Migration Streams

Prior to the 1990s, most international migration in the Southern African region involved young, mostly male, labour migrants moving temporarily to another country to work in primary industry such as mining and commercial agriculture. This form of "circular migration" began in the late nineteenth century and became entrenched in the twentieth.[44] The system was closely regulated by governments and employers who ensured that other family and household members remained behind in the country of origin. Most migrants were warehoused in single-sex dormitories on mines or farms where they were fed high-protein diets by employers.[45] Migrants remitted most of their earnings to rural households who used the funds to pay taxes and purchase basic necessities. Employers paid low wages on the assumption that the rural household would produce food to feed itself. This practice became less tenable as the twentieth century progressed and the sub-continent's rural areas became more degraded and incapable of supporting the population through agriculture. The inevitable result was that in many areas the food security of rural households became increasingly dependent on migrant remittances.

Since 1990, Southern Africa's longstanding regime of temporary cross-border migration has undergone major transformation.[46] The reconfiguration of migration streams has considerable implications for urban and rural food security and the migrants who shuttle between town and country-side. In order to understand the complex inter-relationships between mobility and food security, it is therefore necessary to understand the different types of migration that make up the contemporary migration regime of a region 'on the move.' Firstly, since 1990, there has been a dramatic increase in legal cross-border migration to and within Southern Africa. Traffic between South Africa and the rest of Africa increased from around 1 million in 1990 to nearly 10 million in 2008 (Figure 3). Increased mobility has also been observed at numerous other borders across the SADC region. There are now some migrants from each SADC country in every other SADC country.

FIGURE 3: Legal Entries to South Africa from Rest of Africa, 1990-2010

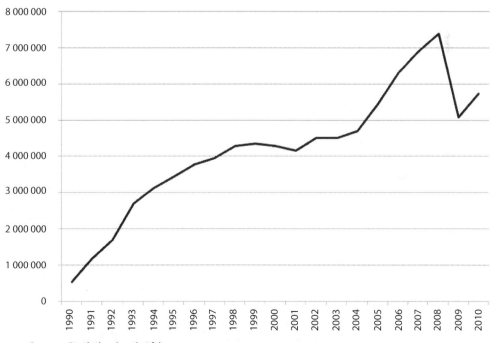

Source: Statistics South Africa

Zimbabwe has become the major migrant sending country in Southern Africa in the last two decades. The vast majority of these migrants are in South Africa with smaller numbers in other SADC countries and in Europe and North America. The number of Zimbabweans crossing legally into South Africa increased from under 200,000 per annum in the late 1980s to 1.5 million in 2010 (Figure 4). In addition, there are an unknown number of undocumented migrants who cross the border through unofficial channels. Zimbabwean migrants maintain very close ties with the country, remitting considerable sums of money and quantities of goods to household members still in the country. Most engage in circular migration and return home frequently. In a 2006 survey, SAMP found that 31% return to Zimbabwe at least once a month and 76% at least once a year.[47]

FIGURE 4: Legal Entries from Zimbabwe to South Africa, 1980-2010

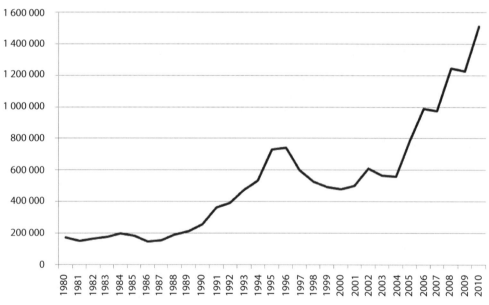

Source: Statistics South Africa

Circular migration is also a defining characteristic of migrants who move to South Africa from other countries in the SADC region. The numbers of migrants from all the other countries in the region have grown consistently since 1994. Those from Malawi, Mozambique and Lesotho come in the greatest numbers. As the Lesotho case demonstrates, this is not just a case of growing numbers but involves complex reconfigurations in who migrates, where and why.[48] For decades, cross-border migration from Lesotho to South Africa was primarily undertaken by young males who went to work on the South African gold mines. This decades-old pattern began to break down in the 1980s and 1990s when the mining industry closed mines and retrenched Basotho migrant workers in considerable numbers. In response, more women began to migrate for work within and outside the country. In South Africa, women tend to work in two sectors known for their lack of regulation and labour rights: commercial farms and domestic work.[49] Within Lesotho, the growth of a domestic textile industry in the country's urban centres has led to a major upsurge in the internal migration of young women (Figure 5).

FIGURE 5: Male Employment in South African Mines and Female Employment in Lesotho Garment Factories, 1990-2006

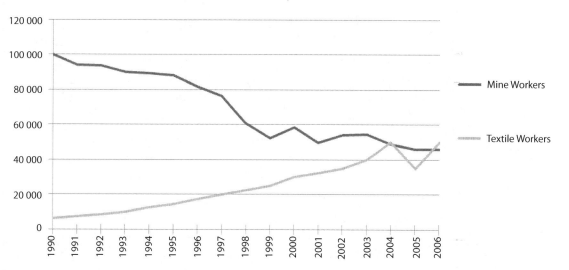

A household survey by SAMP in 2006 in Botswana, Lesotho, Mozambique, Swaziland and Zimbabwe showed that minework in South Africa still constitutes a significant component of the cross-border migration flow (Table 5).[50] The occupational profile of Zimbabwean migrants is far more diverse than migrants from the other countries, with very few mineworkers from that country:

> The contemporary migration flow from Zimbabwe is extremely "mixed" compared with pre-1990 out-migration and with that from other countries in the Southern African region. There are almost as many women migrants as men; there are migrants of all ages from young children to the old and firm; those fleeing hunger and poverty join those fleeing persecution and harassment; they are from all rungs of the occupational and socioeconomic ladder; they are highly-read and illiterate, professionals and paupers, doctors and ditch-diggers.[51]

TABLE 5: Occupations of Labour Migrants in South Africa, 2006						
Occupation	Country of Origin					
	Botswana %	Lesotho %	Mozambique %	Swaziland %	Zimbabwe %	Total %
Professional						
Professional worker	1.6	2.9	1.7	3.5	14.7	4.8
Health worker	0.6	0.3	0.3	0.5	10.6	2.3
Employer/ Manager	0.0	0.0	0.0	0.4	1.3	0.3
Teacher	0.0	0.1	0.1	0.8	7.0	1.5
Farmer	1.1	0.3	0.1	0.4	0.7	0.5
Businessman/ woman	0.6	1.2	4.0	1.1	4.2	2.2
White Collar						
Office Manager	0.3	0.2	0.0	0.8	3.5	0.9
Office Worker	1.1	0.3	0.4	1.7	4.6	1.5
Blue Collar						
Skilled manual	0.8	6.2	8.0	6.1	4.9	5.6
Foreman	0.6	0.1	0.5	0.7	0.5	0.5
Police/Military	0.2	0.0	0.1	0.2	0.4	0.1
Security	0.0	0.2	0.5	1.9	0.1	0.6
Mineworker	87.2	68.4	30.5	62.3	3.0	49.5
Farmworker	0.2	2.0	2.2	0.5	1.2	1.3
Service worker	1.1	1.1	1.2	2.5	9.9	3.1
Unskilled						
Domestic worker	1.7	9.0	0.9	1.6	1.9	3.2
Unskilled manual	0.5	1.5	9.5	7.8	2.1	4.7
Informal Economy						
Informal producer	0.2	2.8	0.8	0.4	4.8	1.8
Trader/ hawker/vendor	0.0	2.0	6.0	0.7	14.7	4.6
Other	0.8	0.0	16.9	4.3	2.9	5.3
N	633	1,076	987	1,132	857	4,685
Source: SAMP Data Base						

Minework is still important for Mozambicans but they, too, have an increasingly diverse occupational profile. In general, however, the migrant stream from all countries is dominated by blue collar, unskilled and informal economy migrants. These migrants come from households in their home countries that are heavily dependent on migrant remittances to meet basic needs and are likely to be more food insecure than their better-resourced counterparts. A central question that therefore needs to be addressed is whether migrant-sending households are more or less food secure than households that do not send migrants. Another important question is the food security experience of migrants themselves at their place of destination. Since many work in low-wage sectors and jobs, and the cost of living is much higher in cities, it is likely that they are also vulnerable to food insecurity when away from home.

The number of labour migrants working without official work permits and/or residency status within the countries of SADC is difficult to determine. Despite very high rates of domestic unemployment, most irregular migrants do seem able to find jobs or income-generating opportunities. A 2010 SAMP study of recent Zimbabwean migrants in South Africa, for example, found that 21% were working in the informal economy, 10% were working part-time and 53% full-time. Only 14% were unemployed.[52] In South Africa, employers in sectors such as commercial agriculture, construction and domestic work actually prefer non-South African workers (since they can subvert labour laws, avoid paying benefits and violate minimum wage legislation).[53] The primary policy response to irregular migration is summary arrest and deportation.[54] Since 1990, just over 3 million migrants have been deported from South Africa (Figure 6). The vast majority (97%) of deportees come from other SADC countries (with Mozambique and Zimbabwe making up 90% of the total), leading some to question the cost effectiveness of this strategy. Deportation in such massive numbers is not generally viewed as a form of "migration" yet it does involve (forced) movement and can have major impacts on the livelihoods and food security of deportees and their households.

FIGURE 6: Deportations from South Africa, 1990-2008

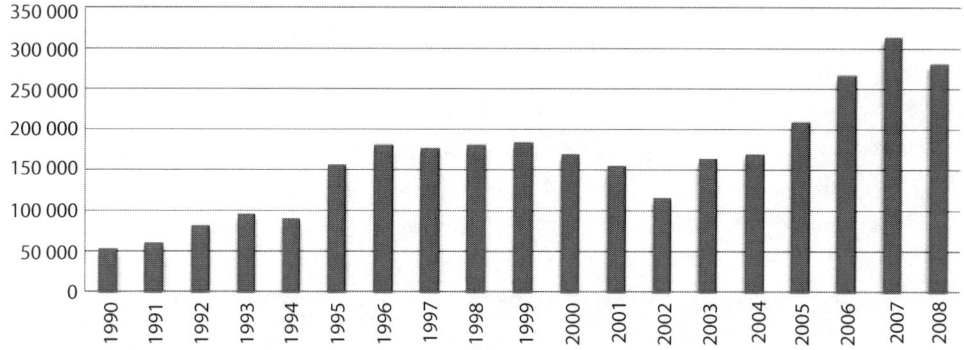

Source: Department of Home Affairs

The SADC region has experienced several waves of mass "forced migration" in recent decades. Over 3 million refugees fled Mozambique in the 1980s to refugee camps in Malawi, South Africa and in Zimbabwe. In South Africa, many refugees eventually settled and were integrated into local rural and urban communities. The war in Angola also led to mass movements of refugees to neighbours Zambia and Namibia. More recently, other "conflict hotspots" in Africa have produced an influx of asylum seekers to the countries of Southern Africa. In South Africa, a total of 150,000 asylum applications were received by the Department of Home Affairs between 1994 and 2004 (Table 6). In the same period, only 27,000 applicants were granted refugee status. In January 2011, the UNHCR estimated that refugee status had been granted to around 53,000 applicants in the whole post-apartheid period. However, the refugee determination process is so backlogged that asylum decisions tend to be taken on the basis of the country of origin rather than the individual circumstances of the claimant. As a result, asylum seekers from countries like Somalia and DRC have found it easier to get refugee status than those from other African countries, such as Zimbabwe.[55]

Since 2004, the number of applications for refugee status has dramatically increased. This is partially because irregular migrants have starting using the system to legitimize their status in South Africa and avoid deportation. In 2009, for example, there were 220,028 new applications for refugee status (Table 7). In that year, 45,538 applications were rejected and only 4,531 were accepted. Of these 75% were from three countries (the DRC, Ethiopia and Somalia). The number of registered asylum seekers in the country at that time was around 420,000. Zimbabwe is now the leading country of refugee claimants in South Africa (149,000 or 68% of all applications in 2009) followed by Malawi (16,000 or 7%). In 2009, only 200 Zimbabweans were granted refugee status while 15,370 applications were refused.

Refugees are permitted by South African law to work and earn income.[56] The situation of asylum-seekers is much more precarious: "Asylum seekers are not allowed to work and thus have no means to support themselves, if they do need support they have to approach government structures. Asylum seekers have no rights to food, work, health care or education."[57] In practice, asylum-seekers have to live and many therefore resort to the informal economy or irregular employment in order to make ends meet while they wait (sometimes interminably) for their claims to be adjudicated. Clearly, though, refugees and asylum seekers do not enjoy the same rights, levels of well-being and possibilities of access to food security.

TABLE 6: Refugee Applications in South Africa by Country of Origin, 1994-2004			
	Country	Applications	
		Number	%
Africa	DRC*	24 808	15.7
	Angola*	12 192	7.7
	Somalia	14 998	9.5
	Nigeria	12 219	7.7
	Kenya	10 553	6.7
	Zimbabwe*	6 857	4.3
	Ethiopia	6 537	4.1
	Tanzania*	4 821	3.1
	Senegal	4 724	3.0
	Burundi	4 570	2.9
	Congo-Brazzaville	3 823	2.4
	Malawi*	2 765	1.8
	Rwanda	2 167	1.4
	Ghana	2 114	1.3
	Cameroon	2 011	1.3
	Ivory Coast	1 006	0.6
Asia	Pakistan	12 576	8.0
	India	10 472	6.6
	Bangladesh	4 173	2.6
	China	2 846	1.8
	Bulgaria	1 616	1.0
	Others	10 098	6.4
Total		157 946	100

* = SADC Countries
Source: Department of Home Affairs

The treatment of migrants in destination countries is another important determinant of income generating opportunities and therefore of individual and household food security. Until recently, anti-immigrant hostility and xenophobia was largely seen as a Northern plague.[58] However, it is becoming increasingly evident that this phenomenon is also increasingly common in migrant-receiving countries in the South.[59] South Africa is one of the most migrant-intolerant countries in the world and xenophobic attitudes and actions are distressingly common.[60] In May 2008, xenophobic violence swept the country's poor urban communities, leaving over 60 people dead and over 100,000 displaced.[61] Damage to the property and businesses of migrants ran into the millions of rands. The violence destroyed the livelihoods of many migrants (who were corralled in makeshift refugee camps) and led to a dramatic increase in personal insecurity and hardship for migrant-sending households in other countries. While this scale of violence has not been repeated, attacks on foreign-owned businesses continue in many areas. The specific connections between xenophobia, disrupted livelihoods and food insecurity have not yet been examined. However, in general, any analysis of the relationship between migration and food security needs to consider the impact of poor and abusive treatment of migrants by citizens, officialdom and employers.

TABLE 7: Refugee Applications and Decisions in South Africa, 2009			
	Applications	Accepted	Refused
Zimbabwe	149,453	200	15,370
Malawi	15,697	0	7,749
Ethiopia	10,715	1,307	3,130
DRC	6,226	779	1,706
Bangladesh	4,923	31	3,310
India	3,632	0	1,045
Somalia	3,580	1,213	638
China	3,327	0	1,634
Congo	3,223	613	1,391
Pakistan	3,196	0	1,770
Nigeria	3,023	0	2,046
Mozambique	2,559	0	882
Tanzania	1,739	0	602
Niger	1,445	0	1,071
Uganda	1,425	20	759
Burundi	1,208	133	367
Zambia	1,000	0	266
Ghana	942	0	648
Cameroon	667	9	429
Kenya	624	0	276
Angola	335	7	132
Rwanda	275	17	68
Lesotho	258	0	54
Eritrea	219	202	71
Senegal	204	0	74
Algeria	133	0	50
Totals	220,028	4,531	45,538
Source: UNHCR			

3.2 Cross-Border Migration and Urban Food Security

The simplest way to examine the relationship between cross-border migration and food security is to ascertain (a) how international migrants address their own food and nutrition needs in the destination country and (b) what happens to the income that they earn while away from home.

The two questions are not unrelated for the amount of money available to send home is to some degree contingent on the food-related expenditures of the migrant in the destination country. This is not as simple as it sounds because the food-related draw on income in the destination country may extend well beyond the individual migrant's own needs. Migrants rarely live alone and their income may often have to support members of "makeshift" households (not all of whose members can find work) as well as second households. One of the recurrent complaints of the partners of male migrants in Lesotho and Mozambique, for example, is that they receive less money because the migrants support second families in South Africa as well.[62]

The Southern African Migration Programme (SAMP) has conducted major household surveys in several SADC countries and provides valuable information on food expenditures in migrant-sending households.[63] Table 8 shows the sources of income for a regional sample of 4,276 households with international migrants. Cash remittances are the most important source of income in all countries with 74% of all migrant-sending households receiving remittances (with as many as 95% in Lesotho and 83% in Zimbabwe). In-country wage employment is a source of income for 40% of households followed by remittances in kind (37%). Remittances in-kind are particularly important in Zimbabwe and Mozambique. At the other end of the spectrum, only 8% of households receive income from the sale of agricultural produce and only 5% receive social grants (mainly in Botswana).

Remittances and in-country employment are easily the most important sources of household income (an average R400 per month for each). However, as noted, far more households receive income from remittances than in-country employment.

TABLE 8: Income Sources of Migrant Households, 2006 (% of Households)						
	Botswana	Lesotho	Mozambique	Swaziland	Zimbabwe	Total
Wage work	87	9	34	46	57	40
Casual work	12	6	13	2	11	8
Remittances – money	76	95	77	64	83	74
Remittances – goods	53	20	65	17	68	37
Sale of farm products	5	2	21	9	3	8
Formal business	5	1	4	3	4	4
Informal business	9	5	23	14	17	12
Pension/ disability grant	19	0.5	3	2	3	5
Gifts	2	1.5	3	3	2	3
Other	1	0	3	1	0.5	1
Source: SAMP						

The vast majority of households (93%) purchase food and groceries with their income (Table 9). No other expenditure category comes close although a significant minority of households pay for cooking fuel, transportation, clothing, utilities, education and medical expenses. A mere 15% spend income on agricultural inputs (mainly in Swaziland). The proportion of households spending remittances on food was over 80%. Average household expenditures on food were R288 per month which is much greater than the amounts spent on other common categories such as transportation, education and medical expenses. The average monthly expenditure of remittances on food was R150 per month. In other words, remittances provided over 50% of average household income spent on food. Without remittances the amount being spent on food would drop precipitously. Remittances are therefore a critical component of food security for migrant-sending households. Unsurprisingly, 82% of households said that remittances were "very important" and another 18% that they were "important" to meeting household food needs.

TABLE 9: Monthly Expenses of Migrant-Sending Households			
Expenditure Item	% of Households Spending Cash Income on Item	% of Households Spending Remittances on Item	Average Monthly Expense (R)
Food and groceries	93	82	288
Housing	9	10	9
Utilities	38	30	36
Clothes	42	52	267
Medical expenses	30	20	24
Transportation	44	34	48
Education	31	52	91
Entertainment	3	3	18
Savings	17	12	200
Fuel	44	6	58
Farming	15	10	434
Building	8	10	576
Special events	8	8	239
Gifts	4	3	55
Other expenses	2	1	81
Source: SAMP			

The study found that 28% of households spend more than 60% of their income on food. This varied considerably from country to country ranging from 13% in the case of Zimbabwe to 40% in the case of Mozambique. Even with remittances, only 17% said that they had always or almost always had enough food in the previous year. Again this varied from country to country with only 2% of households in Zimbabwe saying they always or almost always had enough food. Mozambique returned the highest figure, but still only 24%.

Cash remittances are not the only way in which migration contributes to household security as many migrants also send food back home as part of their in-kind remittance "package." Further proof of the importance of migration to household food security and other basic needs is provided in the types of goods that migrants send home. There was little evidence of luxury goods being sent. Instead, clothing (received by 41% of households) and food (received by 29%) were the items most frequently brought or sent. In the case of Mozambique, 60% of households received food and in Zimbabwe, 45%.

4. MIGRANTS AND FOOD SECURITY

The next question addressed in this paper is whether migrants are more food insecure than longer term residents of the poorer areas of Southern African cities. The question is a difficult one to answer definitively for a number of reasons. First, there is the point already made that the food security of the urban and rural members of a household are inter-linked. One of the main reasons for temporary migration to urban areas is to earn income to remit to rural household members. A migrant in the city may sacrifice their own food security in order to remit and ensure that rural relatives have enough to eat. Secondly, in a region in which the majority of the food consumed by urban households is purchased, the food security of the migrant is highly contingent on their ability to earn income in the urban formal or informal economy. Thirdly, there may be significant differences between internal and cross-border migrants in terms of access to urban employment and other income-generating activity. All of these issues require much further research before we can draw definitive conclusions. However, there is suggestive case study evidence for some cities.

Recent studies of food security and migration in Johannesburg and Windhoek provide an opportunity to compare the food security of internal and international migrant households.[64] The Johannesburg study interviewed 487 households, of whom 60% were internal migrants and the rest international migrants (mainly from Zimbabwe). Three quarters of the internal migrants were living in an informal settlement (compared to only 11% of cross-border migrants). Most of the cross-border migrants (86%) lived in the inner-city often in multi-household flats. Just over half of the households sent money outside the city. Another 21% sent food. Cross-border migrants in the inner-city were more likely to remit cash (60% versus 38% of households) and food (30% versus 6%) than internal migrants in the informal settlement. In terms of food security, 49% said that their food access had improved since moving to Johannesburg while only 19% felt that it had deteriorated. However, cross-border migrants were more likely to report an improvement than internal migrants. The latter were also more likely to report that they had experienced food shortages in the previous year (68% versus 56%). Dietary diversity was also poorer amongst internal migrants. Clearly, migration may mean improved food access but it does not guarantee that shortages will not be experienced. Unreliable income was cited most often by both sets of migrants as the reason for food shortages.

The Windhoek study interviewed a total of 513 migrant heads of household living in formal and informal settlements. The majority (98%) were internal migrants, mostly from the Northern regions of the country. Money is remitted to rural areas by 54% of the respondents, and 90% of the money is sent to rural areas in the North. Neither food nor goods are sent in any quantity although most migrants said that the bulk of the money they sent was spent on food. There was no evidence of any correlation between food insecurity and formal/informal residence. However, there was a significant association between urban food security and the region of origin. Migrants from the North of the country reported decreased food security in Windhoek compared to home, while those from South reported improved food security. This raises an important general point about the relationship between migration and urban food security i.e. that rural areas are far from uniform in their levels of food insecurity. Migrants coming to the cities do not all share the same food security baseline and this, in turn, impacts on their perceptions of food security in the city.

The 2008 AFSUN urban food security baseline survey provides an opportunity for a much broader regional comparison of migrant and non-migrant households in the poorer neighbourhoods of cities. Given the centrality of food purchase to urban food security, access to income is a critical issue. The question, then, is whether established non-migrant households are more or less likely to access regular and reliable sources of income, both formal and informal. In general, the income source profile for migrant and non-migrant households is not that dissimilar (Table 10). Across the sample as a whole, unemployment rates are high with nearly half of both migrant and non-migrant households receiving no income from regular wage work. This suggests that migrants are no more or less likely to obtain wage employment than permanent residents in the city, a finding of some significance since it is often assumed that migrants have a harder time finding work than those born and bred in a city.

Migrant households do seem to find it easier to derive income from casual work (Table 10, Figure 7). A number of other small differences emerged. First, non-migrant households were more involved than migrant households in running informal and formal businesses (20% versus 14%). This suggests it may be easier for permanent residents of the city to access the resources (such as credit) to run and grow a business. Secondly, although very few households in either category earn any income from the sale of home-grown agricultural produce, non-migrant households did seem a little more likely to engage in urban agriculture, presumably because they have readier access to land through home ownership. Thirdly, migrant households were slightly more likely than non-migrant households to be receiving social grant income (19% versus 16%). The difference is not large but it suggests that migrant households eligible to receive social grants are able to access them even if they are not in their home area.

TABLE 10: Sources of Household Income

	Migrant Households (%)	Non-Migrant Households (%)
Wage Work	51.2	54.4
Casual Work	24.2	20.1
Remittances	8.0	8.4
Urban Agriculture Products	1.0	3.2
Formal Business	3.5	4.1
Informal Business	10.5	15.9
Rent	4.0	5.5
Social Grants	19.3	15.6
N	2,425	801

FIGURE 7: Sources of Household Income

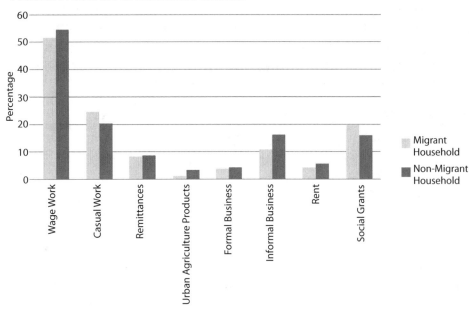

The similarities in the access of migrant and non-migrant households to the labour market and to various income-generating activities suggests that they might have similar income levels and, in turn, levels of food security. In fact, there was one distinct difference in the income profile of migrant and non-migrant households (Figure 8). About a third of the households in each group fell into the lowest income tercile. However,

36% of non-migrant households were in the upper income tercile, compared to only 29% of migrant households. The situation was reversed with the middle income tercile. In other words, migrant status is not a completely reliable predictor of whether a household will be income poor. However, non-migrant households are likely to have a better chance of having better incomes, primarily because some are able to access better-paying jobs.

FIGURE 8: Income Terciles

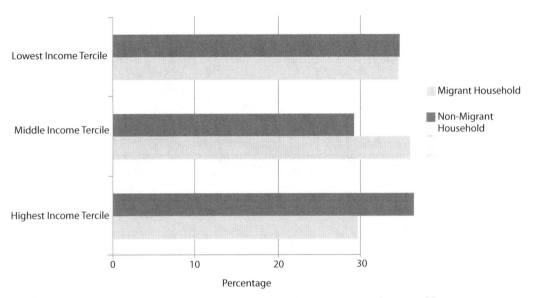

Since urban households purchase the bulk of their food, non-migrant households might have a better chance of being food secure than migrant households. The Household Food Insecurity Scale (HFIAS) measures access to food on a 0 (most secure) to 27 (most insecure) point scale. The mean and median score for all households in the survey was 10, suggesting widespread food insecurity. Individual city means varied from a low of 5 in Johannesburg to a high of 15 in Harare.[65] In terms of the relationship between the HFIAS and food security, migrant households had a mean score of 10.5 and a median of 10. Non-migrant households had lower scores of 8.9 and 8 respectively. Although the differences are not massive, the results confirm that non-migrant households have a better chance of being food secure than migrant households.

This finding is given added weight by the Household Food Insecurity Access Prevalence (HFIAP) Indicator. Only 16% of migrant households can be categorized as "food secure" using the HFIAP Indicator, compared with 26% of non-migrant households (Figure 9). At the opposite end of the scale, 61% of migrant households were severely food insecure, compared with only 48% of non-migrant households. Or again, 78% of migrant households are either moderately or severely food insecure, compared with 65% of non-migrant households. Although levels of food insecurity are disturbingly high for both types of household, migrant households stand a greater chance of being food insecure.

FIGURE 9: Food Security of Migrant and Non-Migrant Households

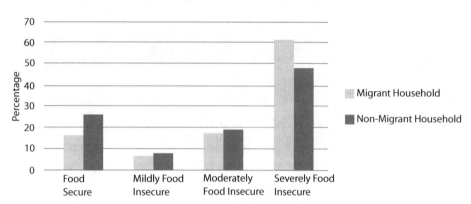

Another dimension of food insecurity is dietary diversity. The Household Dietary Diversity Scale (HDDS) measures how many food groups have been eaten by household members in the previous 24 hours (up to a maximum of 12). Most poor migrant and non-migrant households do not have a particularly diverse diet. For example, nearly half of both groups consumed food from 5 or fewer food groups, and nearly a quarter from 3 or fewer food groups. The main difference between the two groups comes at the other end of the scale where diverse diets are more frequent among non-migrant than migrant households. For example, 28% of migrant households consumed food from 7 or more food groups, compared with 38% of all non-migrant households. In other words, non-migrant households are generally likely to have a more diverse diet.

Another question is whether there are any differences between migrant and non-migrant households in where they obtain their food in the city. Here some interesting differences emerged. Migrant households were more likely than non-migrant households to patronise supermarkets. The opposite was true with regard to the informal food economy. The reason for this difference is not immediately apparent but may have to do with the fact that non-migrant households would be more familiar with alternative food sources compared with recent in-migrants, in particular, who would be more likely to know about and recognise supermarket outlets. A second difference is the extent to which households rely on other households for food, either through sharing meals or food transfers. This was more common among migrant than non-migrant households, suggesting the existence of stronger social networks amongst migrants. Thirdly, and unsurprisingly given their greater degree of access to land for gardens, non-migrant households were more likely to grown some of their own food than migrant households.

TABLE 11: Household Dietary Diversity		
No. of Food Groups	Migrant Households (cum %)	Non-Migrant Households (cum %)
1	3	4
2	14	14
3	24	23
4	34	33
5	47	45
6	59	56
7	71	66
8	83	78
9	91	86
10	95	91
11	97	95
12	100	100

FIGURE 10: Sources of Food for Migrant and Non-Migrant Households

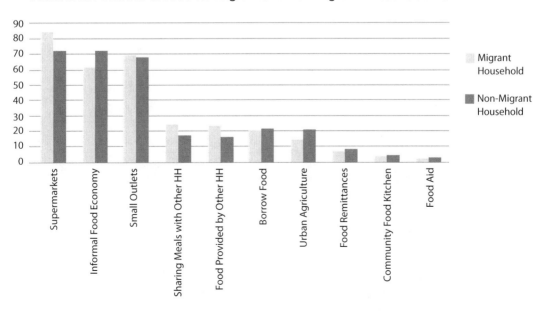

5. MIGRATION AND FOOD TRANSFERS

The rural and urban nodes in stretched households are linked by flows of people, cash, goods and information. There is evidence that urban households in Africa rely to varying degrees on an informal, non-marketed supply of food from their rural (and urban) relatives in order to survive within hostile urban environments.[66] In one documented case, Windhoek, the contribution turned out to be extremely significant.[67] Frayne's study of 305 poor urban households found that poverty was widespread and accompanied by high rates of unemployment. In addition, casual work was not commonly available for low-income residents. The informal sector was much more limited than in other cities in the region and urban agriculture was scant and provided little contribution to household food security. Only 5% of the sample were involved in some form of urban agriculture. Yet there was no widespread starvation and little malnutrition. Only 9% of households said that hunger was always or almost always a problem.

The primary asset that ameliorated the food insecurity of urban households proved to be urban-rural social networks. The resources required to satisfy food and other needs come predominantly from the rural areas direct to the urban household. The most vulnerable households were those that had poor rural connections. However, 98% of the households had relatives in the rural areas. Two-thirds of the households received food from relatives and friends in the year prior to the survey. Nearly 60% received food 2-6 times a year. Another study of Windhoek in 2008 found that 44% of households interviewed in the poorer parts of the city received food from outside the city and that 99% of this food was sent by family members. Furthermore, 73% of this food was sent from the Northern regions. The food received by the urban household included millet, wild foods (especially spinach), meat, poultry and fish. The vast majority of households (90%) consumed the food themselves with only 6% selling it and 4% giving it away to other relatives and friends. In Windhoek, therefore, urban food security for economically marginal households was dependent "to a large degree" on the transfer of food from rural relatives:

> The flow of goods between the urban and rural areas is truly reciprocal. With about two thirds of urban households both sending money to the rural areas and receiving food from rural households, the rural-urban symbiosis is well-established. Unless there is rapid economic growth with jobs for unskilled and semi-skilled workers in

Windhoek, the flow of food into the urban areas is likely to continue as urban households continue to diversify their sources of food and income.[68]

In the case of Maputo, the urban poor maintain "a close and conscious relationship" with their rural area of origin:

> They argue that it is important to maintain relationships with relatives and others in the village, and that being involved in agriculture is important as "we do not have to spend so much money on food." Having *machambas* in the village is considered the best option as this attaches people to their extended family, but many also have small plots on the outskirts of Maputo or in the *bairro* itself.[69]

In Harare, too, migrants to the city maintain strong social and material connections with the rural areas. In the past, the established practice was for urban households to send money and supplementary food to the rural areas. However, economic hardships in the city are now making it difficult for these flows to continue.[70] Many urban households maintain small plots of land in the village where they grow crops or keep animals. The importance of these activities has grown with the food crisis in the cities. By engaging in rural farming, urban household members contribute to generating the food that they eat when they visit the countryside or sell to get a supplementary income that they can use in both the rural and urban area. A 2008 survey in Harare found that 35% of respondents normally visit the rural areas to engage in farming activity.[71] As many as 64% of household respondents also reported that they normally visit their rural homes to collect food and/or money. The economic crisis in that country has, however, reconfigured the nature of these relationships and flows. Urban households are increasingly getting more from the village than they send, suggesting that the flow of resources between the rural and the urban area has reversed. The net urban-ward flow of resources, and especially food, is partly responsible for the resilience of poor households in the city. More than half of the households surveyed (61%) received food from the rural areas. The most common foods transferred from the rural areas included cereals (54% of households), root and tubers (36%), meat and poultry (26%) and food made from beans and nuts (16%) (Figure 11). The high cost of transport between the rural and the urban areas meant that the majority of food transfers were only taking place 3-6 times a year or even less frequently. Another crisis-related response involved members of the urban household migrating back to the rural areas of Zimbabwe.

FIGURE 11: Type and Frequency of Rural-Urban Food Transfers to Harare

% of Households

Kind of food received

| At least once a week | At least once every 2 months | 3–6 times a year | At least once a year |

Source: Tawodzera, 2010.

The prevalence of rural–urban food linkages in other parts of the Southern African region needs more systematic investigation.[72] With this in mind, the 2008-9 AFSUN baseline survey included a number of questions about food transfers in the 11 cities in which the survey was conducted.[73]

Almost one in three of the poor urban households surveyed by AFSUN said they receive food from relatives or friends outside the city. The food flows from relatives make up over 90% of the total. The study confirmed the significance of food transfers in Windhoek with 47% of households receiving food from outside the city. Transfers were also very significant in Lusaka (44%), Harare (42%), Maseru (37%), Blantyre (36%) and Manzini (35%) (Figure 12). By contrast, and not unexpectedly given the impoverished state of South Africa's communal land areas, the proportion of urban households receiving food transfers was much lower in the three South African cities surveyed. While food transfers from rural areas were certainly significant (41% of all households receiving transfers), the survey made the important finding that even more transfers (48%) occurred between households in different urban areas. The remainder received food from both rural and other urban areas. Once again, clear differences emerged between different cities. Households in Windhoek and Gaborone were at one end of the spectrum, with around 70% of transfers emanating from rural areas.

FIGURE 12: Total Food Transfers to Urban Households (% of Households)

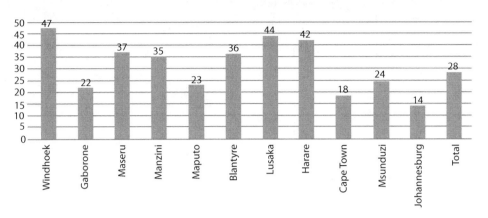

The relative importance of rural–urban versus urban–urban food transfers varied considerably from city to city. Rural transfers to households in Windhoek made up 72% of total transfers while urban–urban transfers made up only 12%. At the other end of the spectrum were the South African cities. Cape Town, for example, had figures of 14% for rural-urban and 83% for urban–urban transfers. Some 82% of transfers to Msunduzi and 62% of transfers to Johannesburg were also from other urban areas outside these cities. The South African pattern reflects several things. First, South Africa is the most urbanized of the nine countries in the study. Secondly, South Africa's rural areas are so impoverished that they do not produce excess food that can be sent to support migrants in the city. And thirdly, social networks and ties between relatives in different cities are strong.

The figures for the cities in major migrant-sending countries are also significant. In Maputo, for example, 62% of transfers are urban–urban. High rates of urban–urban food transfer can also be found in Blantyre (51%), Maseru (44%), Lusaka (44%) and Harare (43%). In each case, it is likely that a large proportion of transfers come in the form of food remittances where migrants working in one city (often in another country) send food to their relatives living in another urban area (often in their home country).

TABLE 12: Food Transfers by City (% of Households)										
	Wind-hoek	Gabo-rone	Manzini	Maseru	Lusaka	Blan-tyre	Harare	Joburg	Maputo	Msun-duzi	Cape Town
Rural-Urban Transfers	72	70	53	49	39	38	37	24	23	15	14
Urban-Urban Transfers	12	16	40	44	44	51	43	67	62	82	83
Urban and Rural Transfers	16	14	7	7	17	12	20	9	15	3	3

The type of transfer, whether rural or urban, was related to the frequency with which urban households receive food. Households receive food transfers far more often when the food comes from an urban area. Around a quarter of households who had received food from other urban areas did so at least once a week (compared to only 5% of households who received rural-urban transfers). Some 76% of households received urban-urban transfers at least once every 2 months, compared to only 40% of households receiving rural-urban transfers (Figure 13). This might suggest that urban-urban networks and support mechanisms are stronger than rural-urban ties. Alternatively, transportation is undoubtedly easier between urban areas and urban-urban transfers are also much less likely to be affected by the seasonal agricultural cycle.

FIGURE 13: Frequency of Food Transfers to Urban Households by Area of Origin (% of Households)

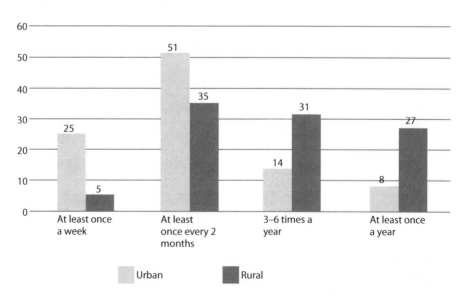

Transfers from rural and other urban areas are both dominated by cereals. All urban households in the study cities received cereals at some point during the year, irrespective of the source. However, there was a marked difference in the frequency of transfers with a quarter of urban-sourced cereals arriving at least once a week and 80% arriving at least once every couple of months or more frequently (Table 13). In contrast, cereals from rural areas came far less frequently, a clear reflection of the rural agricultural cycle. Those receiving cereals from other urban areas are not dependent on the cycle since the cereals can be purchased and sent at any time of the year.

TABLE 13: Frequency of Transfers by Area of Origin (% of Households in Previous 12 Months)			
Food Type	Frequency	Urban (%)	Rural (%)
Cereals	At least once a week	27	2
	At least once every 2 months	52	25
	3-6 times a year	12	36
	At least once a year	9	37
Total		100	100

Other differences between rural and urban transfers also emerged. Households receiving urban transfers were more likely to receive almost all types of foodstuffs (with the exception of foods made from beans, peas, lentils or nuts). For example, 51% of households receiving urban-urban transfers received vegetables compared with 35% of those receiving rural-urban transfers. Or again, 39% of urban-urban transfer households received meat or poultry compared with only 23% of rural-urban transfer households. The differences were particularly marked when it comes to processed foods such as sugar/honey (40% versus 5%) and foods made with oil, fat or butter (33% versus 6%).

Food transfers are particularly important for food-insecure urban households. Of the 1,809 households receiving food transfers from outside the city, 84% were food insecure and 16% were food secure. The relative importance of food transfers for food insecure households holds whether the food is received from rural areas or other urban areas. There were, however, variations between cities. In Gaborone, for example, households were more likely to be food-secure if they receive food from rural sources (33%), compared to either urban only (7%) or combined urban and rural sources (8%). In Maputo, on the other hand, only 1% of food-secure households received food from rural areas only, with 17% of food-secure households getting food from urban areas only (mostly from migrants in South African cities) and the rest from both sources. Around 80% of households receiving food transfers said that they were important or very important to the household while 9% said they were critical to household survival.[74] Almost the same number (77%) said that the food was sent to help the urban household feed itself. Only 20% said the food was sent as a gift. The centrality of food transfers to urban food consumption was illustrated by the fact that only 3% of households receiving food sold it for cash income. The rest consumed the food themselves.[75]

TABLE 14: Types of Food Transferred		
	Rural-Urban % of Receiving Households	Urban-Urban % of Receiving Households
Cereals/grain	100	100
Roots/tubers	21	35
Vegetables	37	51
Fruit	9	19
Meat/poultry	23	39
Eggs	4	14
Food from beans, peas, lentils, nuts	40	30
Cheese/milk products	10	18
Foods made with oil, fat, butter	6	33
Sugar/honey	5	40
N	753	890

As noted above, food transfers from households outside the city to households within it are a notable feature in a number of SADC cities. The final question which the AFSUN data sheds light on is whether migrant households are more or less likely to receive transfers than non-migrant households. Frayne has argued that migrants in the city receive such transfers to keep them going while they search for work or other sources of income. This suggests that migrant households, with their stronger rural ties, would be more likely to receive food from rural households. And so it proved although the difference was not that large. A total of 15% of migrant households received food transfers from rural relatives, compared with only 10% of non-migrant households. Some non-migrant households clearly maintain links with rural areas of sufficient strength to facilitate food transfers. On the other hand, non-migrant households were more likely than migrant households to received food transfers from other urban areas (14% versus 10%). In addition, 61% of those non-migrant households receiving food transfers got them from relatives in other urban areas (compared with only 28% who got them from rural areas). Migrant households were also more likely to receive urban than rural transfers although the difference was not as great (46% versus 43% of the total).

TABLE 15: Types of Transfer as Household Migrant-Status		
	Migrant Households (%)	Non-Migrant Households (%)
Rural-Urban Food Transfers	43	28
Urban-Urban Food Transfers	46	61
Rural and Urban Transfers	11	11

6. CONCLUSION

Migration within and to the Southern African region has changed dramatically in recent decades. All of the evidence suggests that the region is undergoing a rapid urban transition through internal migration and natural population increase. There has also been significant growth in temporary cross-border movement within the region. The implications of the region's new mobility regime for food security in general (and urban food security in particular) need much further exploration and analysis. To what degree is heightened mobility related to problems of food insecurity? Food security shocks and chronic food insecurity can certainly be major motives for migration for income-generating opportunities. War and conflict, particularly in Angola and the DRC, led to the displacement of millions who fled to neighbouring countries. The collapse of the Zimbabwean economy since 2000 has pushed hundreds of thousands of desperate food-insecure people out of the country. The meltdown has affected the poor but has also ravaged the urban middle-class leaving migration as the main "exit option." Chronic poverty and related food insecurity is also partially responsible for the upsurge in post-1990 migration from countries such as Lesotho, Mozambique, Malawi and Swaziland.

Current conceptualisations of the food security crisis in Africa provide an inadequate basis for working at the interface between migration and food security. First, there is the pervasive assumption that food security is primarily a rural problem that will be resolved through technical innovation amongst smallholders (in the guise of a new Green Revolution). What seems to be forgotten in this essentially romantic view of the African rural household is that its food security is not simply, or even mainly, a function of what it does or does not grow for itself. Up and down the continent rural households purchase some or most of their food and they do so with cash that they receive from household members who have migrated to earn income in other places within the country and across borders. The evidence for Southern Africa, at least, is that these rural households do not invest remittances in agriculture but in basic necessities, including food purchase.[76] Rural food security, in other words, may be improved but will not be resolved by current productionist approaches to food security.

A second flawed assumption is that food security in urban areas is about promoting urban agriculture. Urban agriculture can certainly contribute to the food security of some households but it is very far from being a panacea for all.[77] The obsession with urban agriculture may be well-intentioned but it derives from the misplaced idea that increased food production is the key to urban food security. The primary determinant of food insecurity in African cities is not production shortfalls but the lack of access to food and that means the absence of a regular and reliable income with which to purchase it. Even within the poorest areas of the city, access varies considerably from household to household with wage employment, other income-generating activity, the size and structure of the household, the educational level of the household members, access to social grants and being embedded in social networks. This paper has also demonstrated that the migrant status of a household is a key determinant of food security. The differences between migrant and non-migrant households are relatively significant. While there are many poor and food insecure households in both camps, there are more food secure households in the non-migrant group.

A third problematic assumption is that the rural and urban are separate spheres with a deep divide between them. This dualistic view of the world is clearly at odds with the observable web of connections and flows that bind rural and urban spaces together. The concept of the stretched or multi-nodal household attempts to capture the reality that even at the micro-scale, there is regular circulation of people, goods and money between town and countryside. Conceptually and methodologically, this reality means that it is impossible to fully explain the state of food security of urban households without reference to their rural counterparts, and vice-versa. For example, one of the reasons why there are fewer food secure migrant households in the cities may be because, unlike non-migrant households, they remit a portion of their income to rural areas which are in even greater need of the cash. On the other hand, the situation of migrant households would be even more desperate but for relatively widespread intra-household rural-urban transfers of food.

The fourth assumption is that migration and mobility are of limited relevance to food security. There are some recent signs of recognition of the reality that migration and remittances play an important role in the food security strategies of rural households. What tends to be overlooked is the role of migration in the food security of urban households. As this paper shows, the majority of households in poor areas in Southern African cities either consist entirely of migrants or a mix of migrants and non-migrants. Rapid urbanization, increased circulation and growing cross-border migration have all meant that the number of migrants and migrant households in the city has grown exponentially. This is likely to continue for several more decades as urbanization continues. We cannot simply assume that all poor urban households are alike. While levels of food insecurity are unacceptably high amongst all of them, migrant households do have a greater chance of being food insecure with all of its attendant health and nutritional problems. This fact needs to be recognised by policy-makers and acted upon.

ENDNOTES

1 Global Commission on International Migration, *Migration in an Interconnected World: New Directions for Action* (Geneva, 2005); UN General Assembly, "International Migration and Development. Report of the Secretary-General" New York, 2006; S. Castles and R. Wise, eds., *Migration and Development: Perspectives from the South* (Geneva: IOM, 2008); UNDP, *Overcoming Barriers: Human Mobility and Development*, Human Development Report 2009, New York.

2 J. Crush and W. Pendleton, "Remitting for Survival: Rethinking the Development Potential of Remittances in Southern Africa" *Global Development Studies* 5(3-4) (2009): 1-28.

3 B. Frayne and J. Crush, "Urban Food Insecurity and the New International Food Security Agenda" *Development Southern Africa* 28(4) (2011): 527-44.

4 See http://www.agra-alliance.org/

5 A. Lerner and H. Eakin, "An Obsolete Dichotomy? Rethinking the Rural-Urban Interface in Terms of Food Security and Production in the Global South" *Geographical Journal* 177(4) (2011): 311-20; see also A. Champion and G. Hugo, eds., *New Forms of Urbanization: Beyond the Rural-Urban Dichotomy* (Aldershot: Gower, 2004); K. Lynch, *Rural-Urban Interaction in the Developing World* (London: Routledge, 2005).

6 F. Ellis and N. Harris, "Development Patterns, Mobility and Livelihood Diversification" Keynote Paper for DFID Sustainable Development Retreat, University of Surrey, Guildford, 2004, p. 13.

7 M. Tienda, E. Preston-Whyte, S. Findley and S. Tollman, eds., *Africa on the Move: African Migration and Urbanisation in Comparative Perspective* (Johannesburg: Wits University Press, 2006); J. Crush and B. Frayne, eds., *Surviving on the Move:*

Migration, Poverty and Development in Southern Africa (Cape Town and Midrand: SAMP and DBSA, 2010).

8   A. Zezza, C. Carletto, B. Davis and P. Winters, "Assessing the Impact of Migration on Food and Nutrition Security" *Food Policy* 36(1) (2011): 1–6; see also T. Lacroix, "Migration, Rural Development, Poverty and Food Security: A Comparative Perspective" International Migration Institute, Oxford University, 2011.

9   M. Ruel, J. Garrett and L. Haddad, "Rapid Urbanization and the Challenges of Obtaining Food and Nutrition Security" In R. Semba and M. Bloem, eds., *Nutrition and Health in Developing Countries: 2nd Edition* (New York: Humana Press, 2008), pp. 639-57.

10   UN-HABITAT, *The State of African Cities 2010: Governance, Inequality and Land Markets* (Nairobi, 2010), p. 207. The UN-HABITAT data for Southern Africa includes the countries of Angola, Botswana, Lesotho, Mozambique, Namibia, South Africa, Swaziland, Zambia and Malawi but excludes other SADC countries such as the DRC, Malawi and Tanzania.

11   K. Cox, D. Hemson and A. Todes, "Urbanization in South Africa and the Changing Character of Migrant Labour in South Africa" *South African Geographical Journal* 86(1) (2004): 7-16.

12   D. Posel and D. Casale, "Internal Migration and Household Poverty in Post-Apartheid South Africa" In R. Kanbur and H. Bhorat, eds., *Poverty and Policy in Post-Apartheid South Africa* (Pretoria: HSRC Press, 2006), pp. 351-65.

13   P. Kok, M. O'Donovan, O. Bouare and J. Van Zyl, *Internal Migration in South Africa* (Pretoria: HSRC Publishing, 2003); P. Kok and M. Collinson, *Migration and Urbanisation in South Africa* (Pretoria: Statistics South Africa, 2006).

14   South African Cities Network, *State of the Cities Report 2006* (Johannesburg, 2006), p. 2.18.

15   D. Posel and D. Casale, "What Has Been Happening to Internal Labour Migration in South Africa, 1993-1999" *South African Journal of Economics* 71(3) (2003): 455-79; D. Posel, "Moving On: Patterns of Labour Migration in Post-Apartheid South Africa" In Tienda et al, *Africa on the Move*, pp. 217-31; A. Todes, P. Kok, M. Wentzel, J. Van Zyl and C. Cross, "Contemporary South African Urbanization Dynamics" *Urban Forum* 21(3) (2010): 331-48.

16   M. Collinson, S. Tollman, K. Kahn, S. Clark and M. Garenne, "Highly Prevalent Circular Migration: Households, Mobility and Economic Status in Rural South Africa" In Tienda et al, *Africa on the Move*, pp. 194-216; M. Collinson, "Striving Against Adversity: The Dynamics of Migration, Health and Poverty in Rural South Africa" *Global Health Action* 3 (2010).

17   Posel and Casale, "Internal Labour Migration and Household Poverty in Post-Apartheid South Africa" pp. 352-3.

18   D. Posel, "Households and Labour Migration in Post-Apartheid South Africa" *Studies in Economics and Econometrics* 34(3) (2010): 129-41.

19   J. Ferguson, *Expectations of Modernity: Myths and Meanings of Urban Life on the Copperbelt* (Berkeley: University of California Press, 1999).

20   D. Potts, "Counter-Urbanization on the Zambian Copperbelt? Interpretations and Implications" *Urban Studies* 42 (2005): 538-609.

21   Ibid., p. 598.

22   E. Ianchovichina and S. Lundstrom, "What Are the Constraints to Inclusive Growth in Zambia?" World Bank Report, Washington, 2008.

23   C. Mutambirwa and D. Potts, "Changing Patterns of African Rural-Urban Migration and Urbanization in Zimbabwe" *Eastern and Southern African Geographical Journal* 1(1) (1990): 26-39.

24   D. Potts and C. Mutambirwa, "Rural-Urban Linkages in Contemporary Harare: Why Migrants Need Their Land" *Journal of Southern African Studies* 16(4) (1990): 177-98.

25   D. Potts and C. Mutambirwa, "'Basics are Now a Luxury': Perceptions of Structural Adjustment's Impact on Rural and Urban Areas in Zimbabwe" *Environment and Urbanization* 10(1) (1998): 55-76; D. Potts," Urban Unemployment and Migrants in Africa: Evidence from Harare 1985–1994" *Development and Change* 31(4) (2000): 879–910.

26   D. Potts, "'All My Hopes and Dreams are Shattered:' Urbanization and Migrancy in an Imploding Economy – The Case of Zimbabwe" *Geoforum* 37(4) (2006): 536-51; D. Potts, "Internal Migration in Zimbabwe: The Impact of Livelihood Destruction in Rural and Urban Areas" In Crush and Tevera, *Zimbabwe's Exodus*, pp. 79-111.

27   Potts, "Internal Migration in Zimbabwe" p. 101.

28   D. Potts, "'Restoring Order?' The Interrelationships Between Operation Murambatsvina in Zimbabwe and Urban Poverty, Informal Housing and Employment" *Journal of Southern African Studies* 32(2) (2006): 273-91; D. Potts, "City Life in Zimbabwe at a Time of Fear and Loathing: Urban Planning, Urban Poverty, and Operation Murambatsvina" In M. Murray and G. Myers, eds., *Cities in Contemporary Africa* (New York: Palgrave Macmillan, 2007), pp. 265-88; M. Vambe, ed., *The Hidden Dimensions of Operation Murambatsvina* (Harare: Weaver Press, 2008).

29   Crush and Tevera, *Zimbabwe's Exodus*.

30   D. Potts, *Circular Migration in Zimbabwe & Contemporary Sub-Saharan Africa* (Woodbridge: James Currey, 2010).

31   Ibid., p. 29.

32   Ibid., p. 193; D. Potts, "Urban Growth and Urban Economies in Eastern and Southern Africa: Trends and Prospects" In D. Bryceson and D. Potts, eds., *African Urban Economies: Viability, Vitality or Vitiation?* (Basingstoke: Palgrave Macmillan, 2006), pp. 67-106; D. Potts, "Recent Trends in Rural-Urban and Urban-Rural Migration in Sub-Saharan Africa: The Empirical Evidence and Implications for Understanding Livelihood Insecurity" Working Paper No. 6, Department of Geography, King's College, London, 2008.

33   B. Frayne, W. Pendleton, J. Crush, B. Acquah, J. Battersby-Lennard, E. Bras, A. Chiweza, T. Dlamini, R. Fincham, F. Kroll, C. Leduka, A. Mosha, C. Mulenga, P. Mvula, A. Pomuti, I. Raimundo, M. Rudolph, S. Ruysenaa, N. Simelane, D. Tevera, M. Tsoka, G. Tawodzera and L. Zanamwe, *The State of Urban Food Insecurity in Southern Africa*, AFSUN Series No. 2, Cape Town, 2010.

34   Zezza et al., "Assessing the Impact of Migration" p. 2.

35   R. Vargas-Lundius, G. Lanly, M. Villarreal and M. Osorio, *International Migration, Remittances and Rural Development* (Rome: FAO and IFAD, 2008).

36   V. Hosegood and I. Timæus, "Household Composition and Dynamics in Kwazulu

Natal, South Africa: Mirroring Social Reality in Longitudinal Data Collection" In E. Van der Walle, ed., *African Households: Census Data,* (New York: M.E. Sharpe, 2005), pp. 58-77.

37   Ibid., p. 10.

38   C. Tacoli, "The Links Between Urban and Rural Development" *Environment and Urbanization* 15(1) (2003), p. 3.

39   W. Pendleton and B. Frayne, "Migration in Namibia: Combining Macro and Micro Approaches to Research Design and Analysis" *International Migration Review* 35(4) (2001): 1054-85.

40   A. du Toit and D. Neves, "Informal Social Protection in Post-Apartheid Migrant Networks: Vulnerability, Social Networks and Reciprocal Exchange in the Eastern and Western Cape, South Africa" Working Paper No. 2, Programme for Land and Agrarian Studies (PLAAS), University of Western Cape, Bellville, 2009, pp. 19-20; see also S. Bekker, "Diminishing Returns: Circulatory Migration Linking Cape Town to the Eastern Cape" *South African Journal of Demography* 8(1) (2001): 1-8; L. Bank and G. Minkley, "Going Nowhere Slowly? Land, Livelihoods and Rural Development in the Eastern Cape" *Social Dynamics* 31(1) (2005): 1-38; A. du Toit and D. Neves, "In Search of South Africa's 'Second Economy': Chronic Poverty, Economic Marginalisation and Adverse Incorporation in Mt Frere and Khayelitsha" Working Paper No 1, Programme for Land and Agrarian Studies (PLAAS), University of Western Cape, Bellville, 2007; and A. du Toit and D. Neves, "Trading on a Grant: Integrating Formal and Informal Social Protection in Post-apartheid Migrant Networks" Working Paper No. 3, Programme for Land and Agrarian Studies (PLAAS), University of Western Cape, Bellville, 2009.

41   du Toit and Neves, "Informal Social Protection in Post-Apartheid Migrant Networks, pp. 39-40.

42   J. Grest, "Urban Governance, State Capacity and the Informalization of Urban Management in Maputo: Some Thoughts on Poverty, Informalization and Survival in the City" Paper presented at Regional Workshop on South African Cities, Stellenbosch, 2006.

43   J. Crush, B. Dodson, J. Gay, T. Green and C. Leduka, *Migration, Remittances and 'Development' in Lesotho*, SAMP Migration Policy Series No. 52, Cape Town, 2010, p. 12.

44   J. Crush, A. Jeeves and D. Yudelman, *South Africa's Labor Empire* (Boulder: Westview Press, 1991).

45   J. Ward and P. Fleming. "Change in Body Weight and Body Comparison in African Mine Recruits" *Ergonomics* 7(1) (1964): 83-90.

46   J. Crush and V. Williams, *Labour Migration Trends and Policies in Southern Africa*, SAMP Policy Brief No. 23, Cape Town, 2010.

47   Crush and Tevera, *Zimbabwe's Exodus*, p. 13

48   Crush et al., *Migration, Remittances and 'Development' in Lesotho*.

49   T. Uliki and J. Crush, "Poverty, Gender and Migrancy: Lesotho's Migrant Farmworkers in South Africa" *Development Southern Africa* 24(1) (2007): 155-72; L. Griffin, "Unravelling Rights: 'Illegal' Migrant Domestic Workers in South Africa" *Southern African Review of Sociology* 42(2) (2011): 83-101.

50   W. Pendleton, J. Crush, E. Campbell, T. Green, H. Simelane, D. Tevera and

F. De Vletter, *Migration, Remittances and Development in Southern Africa*, SAMP Migration Policy Series No. 44, Cape Town, 2006.

51   Crush and Tevera, *Zimbabwe's Exodus*, p. 9.

52   J. Crush, A. Chikanda and G. Tawodzera, *The Third Wave: Mixed Migration from Zimbabwe to South Africa*, SAMP Migration Policy Series No. 59, Cape Town, 2012.

53   B. Rutherford, "An Unsettled Belonging: Zimbabwean Farm Workers in Northern South Africa" *Journal of Contemporary African Studies* 26(4) (2008): 401-15; T. Ulicki and J. Crush, "Poverty, Gender and Migrancy: Lesotho's Migrant Farmworkers in South Africa" In Crush and Frayne, *Surviving on the Move*, pp. 164-82; N. Dinat and S. Peberdy, "Worlds of Work, Health and Migration: Domestic Workers in Johannesburg" In Crush and Frayne, *Surviving on the Move*, pp. 215-34; T. Araia, S. Kola and T. Polzer Ngwato, "Migration and Employment in the Construction Industry" ACMS Research Report, Wits University, Johannesburg, 2010; J. Vearey, E. Oliveira, T. Madzimure and B. Ntini, "Working the City: Experiences of Migrant Women in Inner-City Johannesburg" *Southern Africa Media and Diversity Journal* 9 (2011): 228-33.

54   R. Amit, "Lost in the Vortex: Irregularities in the Detention and Deportation of Non-Nationals in South Africa" FMSP Research Report, Wits University, Johannesburg, 2010; R. Sutton and D. Vigneswaran, "A Kafkaesque State: Deportation and Detention in South Africa" *Citizenship Studies* 15(5) (2011): 627-42.

55   D. Vigneswaran, "A Foot in the Door: Access to Asylum in South Africa" *Refuge* 25(2) (2009): 41-52.

56   D. Vigneswaran, "The Revolving Door: Asylum Seekers, Access and Employment in South Africa" In S. Gallo-Mosala, ed., *Migrants' Experiences Within the South African Labour Market* (Cape Town: Scalabrini Centre, 2009).

57   T. Dalton-Greyling, "Refugees and Forced Migrants in South Africa's Urban Areas: Definitions, Rights, Levels of Wellbeing and Policy" TIPS Annual Forum, Johannesburg, 2008.

58   J. Fetzer, *Public Attitudes Toward Immigration in the United States, France, and Germany* (Cambridge: Cambridge University Press, 2000); J. Roemer, W. Lee and K. Van der Straeten, *Racism, Xenophobia, and Distribution: Multi-Issue Politics in Advanced Democracies* (Cambridge: Harvard University Press, 2007); R. Taras, *Europe Old and New: Transnationalism, Belonging, Xenophobia* (Lanham MD: Rowman & Littlefield, 2009).

59   J. Crush and S. Ramachandran, "Xenophobia, International Migration and Development" *Journal of Human Development and Capabilities* 11(2) (2010): 209-28.

60   J. Crush, D. McDonald, V. Williams, K. Lefko-Everett, D. Dorey, D. Taylor and R. la Sablonniere, *The Perfect Storm: The Realities of Xenophobia in Contemporary South Africa*, SAMP Migration Policy Series No 50, Cape Town, 2008; D. Everett, "Xenophobia, State and Society in South Africa, 2008-2010" *Politikon* 38(1) (2011): 7-36.

61   Ibid.

62   Crush et al., *Migration, Remittances and 'Development' in Lesotho*.

63   Pendleton et al., *Migration, Remittances and Development in Southern Africa*; F. de Vletter, "Migration and Development in Mozambique: Poverty, Inequality and

Survival" *Development Southern Africa* 24(1) (2007): 137-54; B. Dodson, *Gender, Migration and Remittances in Southern Africa*, SAMP Migration Policy Series No. 49, Cape Town, 2008.

64   J. Vearey, L. Núñez and I. Palmary, "HIV, Migration and Urban Food Security: Exploring the Linkages" Report for RENEWAL Forced Migration Studies Programmes, Wits University, Johannesburg 2009; D. Ashton, J. Mushaandja and A. Pomuti, "The Inter-Relationships and Linkages among Migration, Food Security and HIV/AIDS in Windhoek, Namibia" Report for RENEWAL, University of Namibia, Windhoek, 2009.

65   Frayne et al, *The State of Urban Food Insecurity in Southern Africa,* p. 28.

66   C. Tacoli, "Rural-Urban Interactions: A Guide to the Literature" *Environment and Urbanization* 10(1) (1998): 147-66.

67   B. Frayne, "Survival of the Poorest: Food Security and Migration in Namibia" PhD Thesis, Queen's University, 2001; B. Frayne, "Survival of the Poorest: Migration and Food Security in Namibia" In Mougeot, *Agropolis*, pp. 31-50; B. Frayne, "Migration and the Changing Social Economy of Windhoek, Namibia" *Development Southern Africa* 24(1) (2007): 91-108.

68   Frayne, "Survival of the Poorest", p. 278.

69   M. Paulo, C. Rosário and I. Tvedten, "Xiculongo: Social Relations of Urban Poverty in Maputo, Mozambique" Report No. 13, Chr. Michelsen Institute, Bergen, Norway, 2007, p. 54.

70   Potts, *Circular Migration in Zimbabwe*.

71   G. Tawodzera, "Vulnerability and Resilience in Crisis: Urban Household Food Insecurity in Harare, Zimbabwe" PhD Thesis, University of Cape Town, 2010.

72   For other examples see W. Smit, "The Rural Linkages of Urban Households in Durban, South Africa" *Environment and Urbanization* 10(1) (1998): 77-87; F. Kruger, "Taking Advantage of Rural Assets as a Coping Strategy for the Urban Poor: The Case of Rural-Urban Interrelations in Botswana" *Environment and Urbanization* 10(1) (1998): 119-34; J. Andersson, "Reinterpreting the Rural-Urban Connection: Migration Practices and Socio-Cultural Dispositions of Buhera Workers in Harare" *Africa* 71(1) (2001): 82-112.

73   Frayne et al, *The State of Urban Food Insecurity in Southern Africa*.

74   Ibid., p. 45.

75   Ibid., p. 46.

76   Crush and Pendleton, "Remitting for Survival."

77   J. Crush, A. Hovorka and D. Tevera, "Food Security in Southern African Cities: The Place of Urban Agriculture" *Progress in Development Studies* 11(2011): 285-305.

Printed in the United States
By Bookmasters